Promised Land

Early American Hymns from the Shape-Note Tradition

The Rev. Peter B. Irvine

Cover artwork named "An American Autumn" by Susan Hunt-Wulkowicz

WWW.MELBAY.COM

Dedication

"Brightest and best are the sons of the morning"

remembering a hymn singer I have known

Harry Lee Eskew

By Peter B. Irvine

December 12, 2020

During these dark days of the pandemic, when more people have died in 2020 than anyone could have imagined, I remember the friends, relatives and teachers who taught me to sing with love and understanding. My teacher and friend Harry Eskew died most recently, on the first Sunday of Advent. I met Harry at a conference of The Hymn Society in Ottawa, the summer of 2007, and saw him at society conferences 2008-2010, finally visiting him at his home in Macon, Georgia, a few years later.

Harry had written a masters thesis on *Southern Harmony,* the shape-note hymn book published by William Walker in 1835. At the time I met him, I was in the process of producing an online edition, and I approached him with some trepidation, as I was not sure how Harry would receive this idea. He was most encouraging, and later agreed to contribute an introduction to the online edition.

What I remember best about the time I spent with Harry was when the Hymn Society had its conference in Birmingham, Alabama, and Harry invited me to visit the Sixteenth Street Baptist Church with him. I was quite young when the church had been bombed by members of the Ku Klux Klan in 1963, shortly after the March on Washington led by Martin Luther King and others. Visiting the church with Harry helped me to remember that terrible year, which culminated with the assassination of President John F. Kennedy. Had Harry not reminded me of this dark history, I am not sure I would ever have gotten it straight.

A few years later, I visited Harry and his wife Margaret at their home in Macon, Georgia, and we went to visit Andersonville, the site of the most notorious prison of the Civil War. Like our previous experience together in Birmingham, this visit was strangely healing, as we re-visited the terrible past of these two places, which have stained the history of this country with blood, both real and metaphorical. Now that we are about to turn the page on yet another of the darkest years of history, I remember Harry and his ability to confront some of the most horrendous events of our lifetime with serenity, faith, and hope. Harry taught me and so many others to sing not only with understanding, but with love.

Table of Contents

Title **Page**

Foreword - A Personal History of Shape-Note Singing

The Sacred Harp:

A Bond of Kindred Spirits

United by the "Sacrament of Hymnody"

By Peter B. Irvine

In 1971, my cousin Philip Taber introduced me to *The Sacred Harp,* a book of shape-note hymns that had just been issued in a revised edition. I recall being in my grandmother's house, in the parlor where the Steinway grand piano stayed, when Philip came by to give his Aunt Margaret (my grandmother) a copy of the new book. I was deeply interested in music at that point, and was intrigued by the various shapes used in the book's notation: triangle, ellipse, rectangle, and diamond, corresponding to the syllables Fa, Sol, La, and Mi.

A few years later, I found myself sojourning in Atlanta, Georgia, where I fell in with a performing arts company called Kelly's Seed & Feed Theatre. The group had two adjunct musical ensembles: the Abominable Marching Band and the Schola Cantorum. The Schola had been formed when the theatre hosted a concert by the Word of Mouth Chorus from Vermont. The Chorus had given a set of 1971 *Sacred Harp* books to the Atlanta group, which proceeded to learn quite a few of the four-part hymns, singing them with gusto and finesse. This was the first time I heard the *Sacred Harp* sung, and it made an indelible impression on me. I later went with the Schola to a country church for a traditional singing, which lasted all day and included a pot-luck picnic on the church grounds.

Everywhere I go, it seems, I run into *Sacred Harp* singers, including Atlanta, Chattanooga (my hometown), Pittsburgh, Madison, Fond du Lac, Janesville, and Chicago. In each of these places, I have received a warm welcome, not through any merit of mine, but because *Sacred Harp* singers are quick to welcome newcomers. Although in 2020, almost all singings were cancelled due to the COVID-19 pandemic, singers have found ways to keep in touch with one another. Some have organized online singings, and others have adapted the music for singing solo at home while quarantined. This book is intended for people who like to sing shape-note music with the accompaniment of instruments. This type of arrangement is very different from the four-square gatherings of singers we are used to, but it provides a way to keep in touch with the music for those who are confined at home or just want to try another way of singing it.

Some of the music of the *Sacred Harp* dates back to the colonial period, when William Billings was one of the most prominent composers of the New England school. In 1835, William Walker published *Southern Harmony,* a three-part shape-note hymnal that is still used in its original form almost two hundred years later. T*he Sacred Harp,* originally published in 1844, has been revised with the addition of new compositions, most recently in 1991. Another version, the *Cooper Book*, was published in a revised edition in 2012.

Shape-note music has a primitive, folk-like quality, as exemplified by the tunes from *Southern Harmony* complied in the 1982 Hymnal of the Episcopal Church; *Kedron, Star in the East, Middlebury, Holy Manna, Wondrous Love, Restoration* and *Charlestown.* These are just a few of the sturdy, distinctly American tunes of shape-note music.

What unites *Sacred Harp* singers everywhere is the importance of music in all of their meetings. Although these often take place in church buildings, they have their own liturgy, which revolves around the singing of hymns, chosen in a egalitarian fashion that allows anyone to choose a hymn to be sung who wishes to do so. Likewise, the person who chooses the hymn has the privilege of pitching the notes and beating time. Records of who attends, who directs, and who chooses which tune are faithfully kept and published in a yearly minute book. The singing has become the sacrament. Unlike traditional churches, *Sacred Harp* meetings do not baptize converts or celebrate the Holy Eucharist: words, music, and singers, inextricably tied together, are the "outward sign of inward grace."

At a time when traditional churches are sometimes embroiled with controversy or bogged down in trying to grow their membership, the *Sacred Harp* provides a welcome antidote in transforming people and spreading the faith strictly through singing. As the Chicago Sacred Harp Singers say, "We don't rehearse. We don't perform. We just *sing."* Typically, *Sacred Harp* singers stay away from arguments about religion, doctrine, or politics: they sing for the sake of singing itself, and for many of us, that is a spiritual breath of fresh air.

All Is Well

In honor of Johanna Fabke

Anonymous

Jesse T. White

G D Emin Bmin Amin
1. What's this that steals, that steals up - on my
2. Weep not my friends, my friends weep not for
4
G Dsus D G
frame? Is it death? Is it death?
me, All is well! All is well!
G D Emin Bmin Amin
7
That soon will quench, will quench this mor - tal
My sins for - giv'n, for - giv'n and I am
G Dsus D G
10
flame? Is it death? Is it death?
free, All is well! All is well!
G Emin C
13
If this be death I soon shall be,
There's not a cloud that doth a - rise,
Dsus Bmin D
16
From ev - 'ry pain and sor - row free,
To hide my Je - sus from my eyes,
Bmin Dsus Emin Bmin
19
I shall the King of glo - ry see. All is
I soon shall mount the up - per skies. All is
Amin Dsus G
22
well! All is well!
well! All is well!

Bozrah

In honor of Alora Young

Joshua Spalding

Southern Harmony

Bmin D A F♯min Bmin F♯sus Bmin
1. Who is this that comes from far, With his gar - ments dipp'd in blood,

Bmin D A F♯min Bmin F♯sus Bmin
5
Strong, tri - um - phant tra - vel - ler Is he man, or is he God?

Bmin Bmin F♯min D A D A
9
I that reign in right - eous - ness, Son of God and man I am;

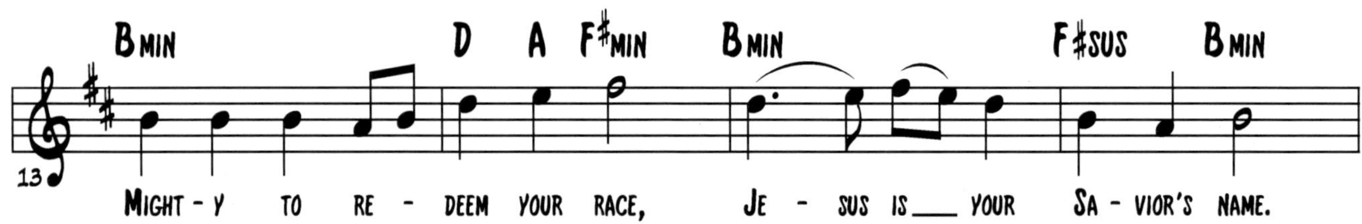

Bmin D A F♯min Bmin F♯sus Bmin
13
Might - y to re - deem your race, Je - sus is ___ your Sa - vior's name.

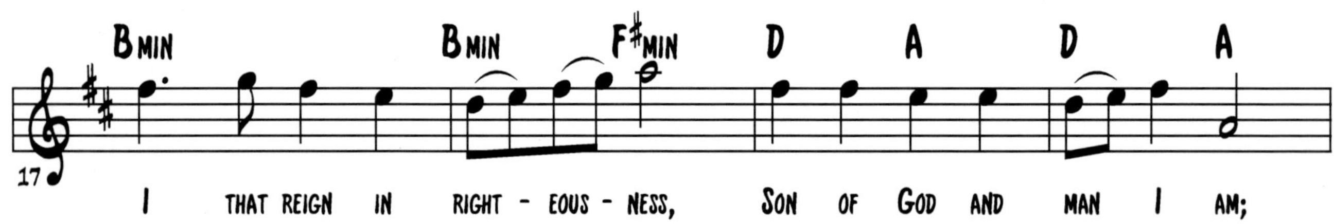

Bmin Bmin F♯min D A D A
17
I that reign in right - eous - ness, Son of God and man I am;

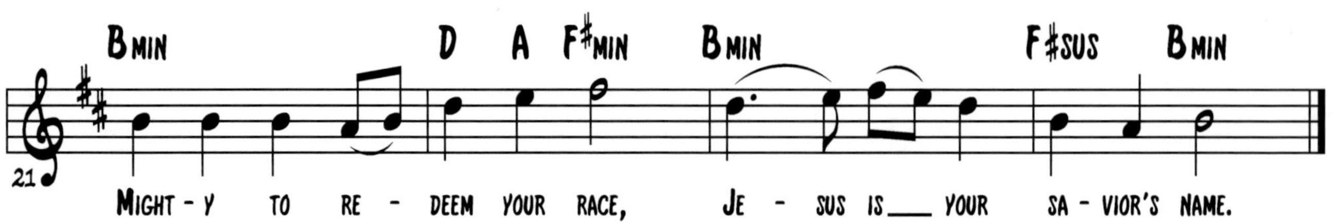

Bmin D A F♯min Bmin F♯sus Bmin
21
Might - y to re - deem your race, Je - sus is ___ your sa - vior's name.

Consolation

Isaac Watts

Elkanah Kelsey Dare

E min
B min
1. Once more, my soul, the ___ ri - sing ___
2. Night un - to night his ___ name re -
3. Dear God, let all my ___ hours be ___
4
E min D C D G
day sa - lutes thy wak - ing eyes;
peats, The day re - news the sound.
thine, Whilst I en - joy the light,
8
G D B min
Once ___ more, my ___ voice, thy tri - bute ___ pays
Wide ___ as the ___ heav'ns on which he ___ sits,
Then ___ shall my ___ sun in smiles de - cline,
12
E min D C D E min
to him that rules ___ the skies. ___
To turn the sea - sons round. ___
And bring a pleas - ing night. ___
16
G D B min
Once ___ more, my ___ voice, thy tri - bute ___ pays
Wide ___ as the ___ heav'ns on which he ___ sits,
Then ___ shall my ___ sun in smiles de - cline,
20
E min D C D E min
to him that rules ___ the skies. ___
To turn the sea - sons round. ___
And bring a pleas - ing night. ___

David's Lamentation

In honor of James Page

2 Samuel 18:33

William Billings

B MIN
A
B MIN
1. Da - vid the King was griev - ed and mov - ed, he went to his

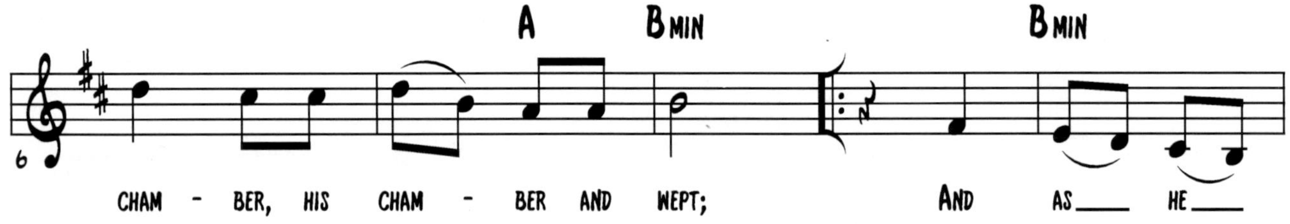
A
B MIN
B MIN
6
cham - ber, his cham - ber and wept; And as ___ he ___

D
A
D
11
went he wept ___ and said, O my son!

D
A
B MIN
B MIN
16
O my son! Would to God I had

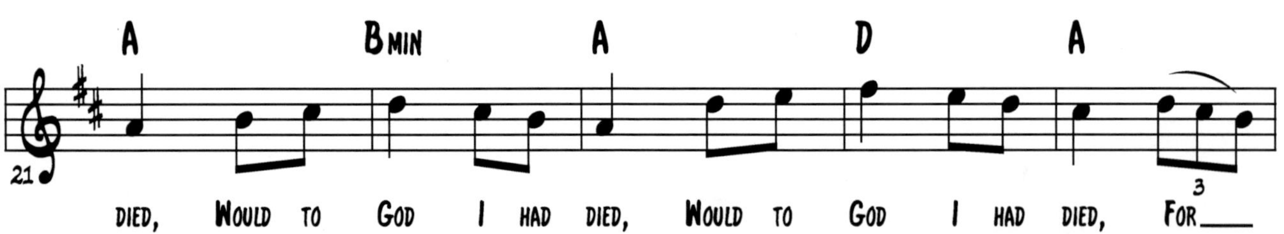
A
B MIN
A
D
A
21
3
died, Would to God I had died, Would to God I had died, For ___

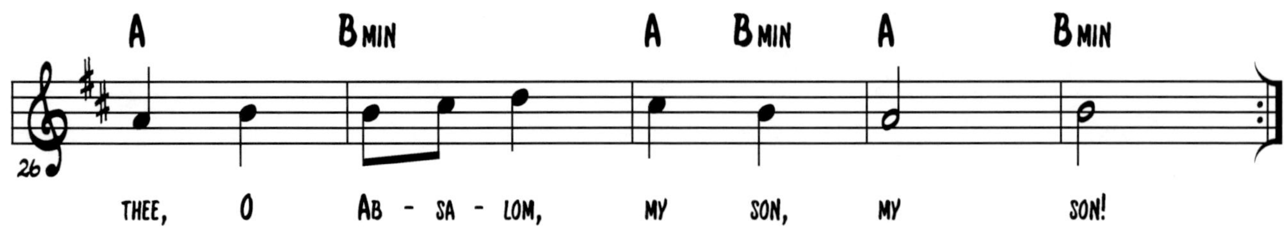
A
B MIN
A
B MIN
A
B MIN
26
thee, O Ab - sa - lom, my son, my son!

Dundee (Norwich Tune)

Julian of Norwich
paraphrase by PBI

Thomas Ravenscroft

D F♯min
1. Lord, on - ly Thou knows't
2. God, of Thy good - ness,
3. And if I ask for
A G D
4
what I wish, if
give Thy - self, Thou
some - thing less, I'll
Bsus Asus D
7
it should be Thy will.
art e - nough to me:
e - ver want with - al:
D G
10
If it be not, be
I can ask no - thing
for by Thee on - ly
Esus A D
13
not dis - pleased, for
that is less to
am I blessed, and
Bsus Asus D
16
I shall love Thee still.
ful - ly hon - or Thee.
in Thee, I have all.

Evening Shade

In honor of Bill Bay

John Leland

Stephen Jenks

Emin D Emin D
1. The day___ is past and gone. The eve - ning shades ap -
2. We lay___ our gar - ments by. U - pon our beds to___
3. Lord, keep___ us safe this night, Se - cure from all our___
4. And when___ we ear - ly rise, And view th'un - wea - ried
5. And when___ our days are past, And we from time re -
Bmin Emin Emin
pear; O___ may___ we___ all re - mem - ber well re - mem - ber well,___ O
rest; So___ death will soon dis - robe us all dis - robe us all,___ So
fears; May an - gels guard us while we sleep, may an - gels guard___ May
sun, May we___ set out to win the prize, And af - ter run___ May
move, O___ may___ we___ in thy bo - som rest, And may we rest,___ And
G Bmin Emin D Emin
may we all re - mem - ber___ well the night of death is near. O___
death will all dis - robe us___ all Of what we here pos - sess. So___
an - gels guard us while we___ sleep, 'Till morn - ing light ap - pears. May
we set out to win___ the___ prize, And af - ter glo - ry run. May
may we in thy bo - som___ rest, The bo - som of___ thy love. And
Emin Emin
may___ we___ all re - mem - ber well re - mem - ber well,___ O
death will___ soon dis - robe us all dis - robe us all,___ So
an - gels___ guard us while we sleep, 'Till___ morn - ing light___ May
we___ set___ out to win the prize, and___ af - ter run___ May
may___ we___ in thy bo - som rest, And___ may___ we rest___ And
G Bmin Emin D Emin
may we all re - mem - ber___ well the night of death is near.
death will soon dis - robe us___ all of what we here pos - sess.
an - gels guard us while we___ sleep, 'Till morn - ing light ap - pears.
we set out to win___ the___ prize, and af - ter glo - ry run.
may we in thy bo - som___ rest, The bo - som of___ thy love.

Fairfield

Edmund Jones | Hitchcock

Bmin
F♯min
Bmin
1. Come, hum - ble sin - ner, in whose breast A thou - sand thoughts re - volve; Come,
2. I'll go to Je - sus, though my __ sin Hath like a __ moun - tain rose; I
3. Per - haps He may ad - mit my __ plea, Per - haps will hear my prayer; But,
4. I can but per - ish if I __ go; I am re - solved to try; For

Bmin
A
G
F♯min
5
with your guilt and fear opp - ress'd, And make this last re - solve. Come,
know His courts, I'll en - ter in, What - e - ver may op - pose; I
if I per - ish, I will pray, And per - ish on - ly __ there; But,
if I stay a - way, I know I must for - e - ver die; For

Bmin
A
F♯min
Bmin
9
with your guilt and fear opp - ress'd And make this last re - solve.
know His courts, I'll en - ter in, What - e - ver __ may op - pose.
if I per - ish, I will pray, And per - ish __ on - ly there.
if I stay a way, I know I must for - e - ver die.

Greenland

Swan

G Gsus C

1. Why should I be af - fright - ed At pes - ti - lence and war, The
2. With Je - sus in the ves - sel, The bil - lows rise in vain, They
3. This world is full of dan - gers, And foes that press me hard; But
4. Here I shall not be temp - ted A - bove what I can bear, When
5. From him I have my or - ders, And while I do o - bey, I
6. The way is so de - light - ful, I wish to tra - vel on, Till

D G D6 G

fierc - er be the tem - pest, The soon - er it is o'er, The
on - ly will con - vey me To you E - ly - sian plains, To
Je - sus he has pro - mised That he will be my guard. That
fight - ings are ex - er - ted, His king - dom for to share. His
find his ho - ly spi - rit Il - lum - i - nates my way. Il -
I ar - rive at hea - ven, T're - ceive a star - ry crown. T're -

G Gsus C

soon - er it is o'er, The soon - er it is o'er, The
you E - ly - sian plains, To you E - ly - sian plains, They
he will be my guard, That he will be my guard, But
king - dom for to share, His king - dom for to share, When
lum - i - nates my way, Il - lum - i - nates my way. I
ceive a star - ry crown, T're - ceive a star - ry crown, Till

D G D6 G

fierc - er be the tem - pest, The soon - er it is o'er.
on - ly will con - vey me To you E - ly - sian plains.
Je - sus he has pro - mised That he will be my guard.
fight - ings are ex - er - ted, His king - dom for to share.
find his ho - ly spi - rit Il - lu - mi - nates my way.
I ar - rive at hea - ven T're - ceive a star - ry crown.

Holy Manna

In honor of Dick Dunagan

George Askins

William Moore

A E A E A
1. Breth-ren, we have met to__ wor - ship, And a - dore the Lord our God; Will you
2. Breth-ren, see poor sin - ners round you, Trem - bling on the Brink of woe; Death is__
3. Let us__ love our God sup reme - ly,__ Let us__ love each oth - er, too; Let us__
E A E A
5
pray with all your pow - er,__ While we__ try to preach the Word? All is
com - ing, hell is__ mo - ving, Can you bear to let them go? See our
love and pray for__ sin - ners, Till our God makes all things new, Then he'll
A E A E A
9
vain un - less the__ Spi - rit of the Ho - ly One comes down; Breth - ren__
fath - ers, see our__ mo - thers, And our chil - dren sink - ing__ down; Breth - ren,
call us home to__ hea - ven, At His tab - le, we'll sit__ down; Christ will
E A E A
13
pray and ho - ly__ man - na__ will be__ show - ered all a - round. All is
pray, and ho - ly__ man - na__ will be__ show - ered all a - round. All is
gird Him - self, and__ serve us__ With sweet man - na all a - round. Then he'll
A E A E A
17
vain un - less the__ Spi - rit of the Ho - ly One comes down; Breth - ren__
vain un - less the__ Spi - rit of the Ho - ly One comes down; Breth - ren__
call us home to__ hea - ven, At His tab - le, we'll sit__ down; Christ will
E A E A
21
pray and ho - ly__ man - na__ will be__ show - ered all a - round.
pray and ho - ly__ man - na__ will be__ show - ered all a round.
gird Him - self, and__ serve us__ with sweet man - na all a - round.

Idumea

In honor of Kelly Morris

Charles Wesley

Ananias Davisson

Emin Dsus Emin G
1. And am I___ born to___ die? To lay this___
2. A land of___ deep - est___ shade, un - pierced by___
3. Soon as from earth I___ go, What will be -
4. Waked by the___ trum - pet___ sound, I from my___
6
Emin Bmin G Emin
bo - dy down? And must my___ trem - bling___
hu - man thought; The Drea - ry___ reg - ions___
come of me? E - ter - nal___ hap - pi -
grave shall rise; And see the___ Judge with___
10
Bmin Emin Dsus
spi - rit___ fly in - to a___ world un -
of the___ dead, Where all things are for -
ness or___ woe Must then my___ por - tion___
glo - ry___ crowned, And see the___ flam - ing___
14
Emin G Emin
known? And must my___ trem - bling___ spi - rit___
got! The drear - ry___ reg - ions___ of the___
be! E - ter - nal___ hap - pi - ness or___
skies! And see the___ Judge with___ glo - ry___
18
Bmin Emin Dsus Emin
fly in - to a___ world un - known?
dead, Where all things are for - got!
woe Must then my___ por - tion___ be!
crowned, And see the___ flam - ing___ skies!

Jesus Wept (When)

William Billings

1. When Je - sus wept the fall - ing tear in
5
mer - cy flowed be - yond all bounds; when
9
Je - sus groaned a trem - bling tear seized
13
all the guilt - y world a - round.

Kedron

In honor of Linda Warren

Charles Wesley

Amos Pilsbury, Compiler

Emin G D Emin Bmin
1. Thou man of grief re - mem - ber me,
2. Fa - ther, if I may call thee so,
3. I trem - ble, lest the wrath di - vine,
Emin D G C Bmin
Who ne - ver canst thy - self for - get,
Re - gard my fear - ful heart's de - sire;
Which bruis - es now my wret - ched soul.
Emin G G Emin G Dsus
Thy last ex - pi - ring a - go - ny,
Re - move this load of guil - ty woe,
Should bruise this wret - ched soul of mine,
D Emin C D Emin
thy faint - ing pangs and blood - y sweat.
nor let me in my sins ex - pire!
Long as e - ter - nal ag - es roll.
Emin G G Emin G Dsus
thy last ex - pi - ring a - go - ny,
Re - move this load of guil - ty woe,
Should bruise this wret - ched soul of mine,
D Emin C D Emin
thy faint - ing pangs and blood - y sweat.
nor let me in my sins ex - pire!
Long as e - ter - nal ag - es roll.

Lone Pilgrim

In honor of Richard Ackley

John Ellis

Thomas Commuck

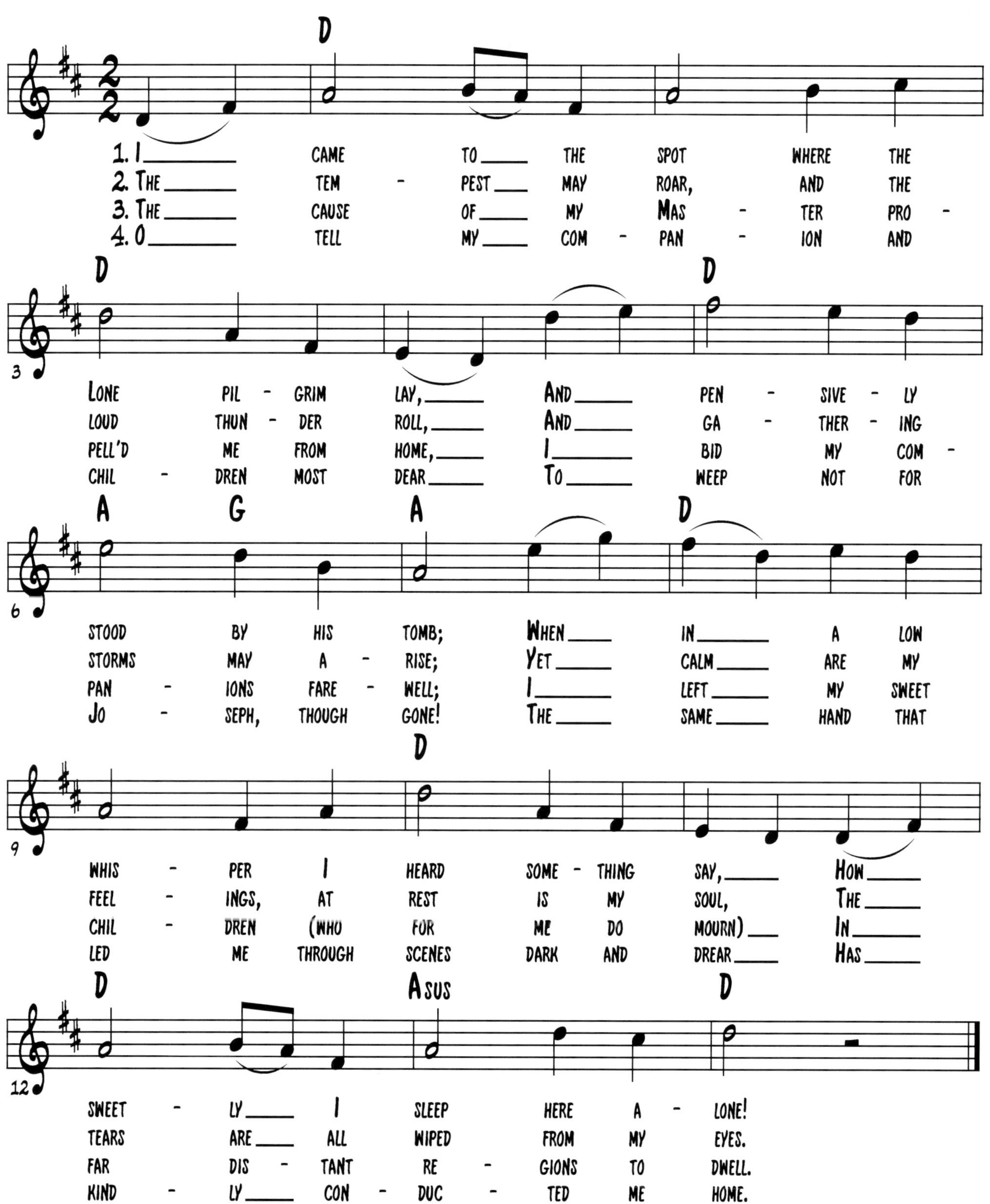
D
1. I came to the spot where the
2. The tem - pest may roar, and the
3. The cause of my Mas - ter pro -
4. O tell my com - pan - ion and
D D
Lone pil - grim lay, And pen - sive - ly
loud thun - der roll, And ga - ther - ing
pell'd me from home, I bid my com -
chil - dren most dear To weep not for
A G A D
stood by his tomb; When in a low
storms may a - rise; Yet calm are my
pan - ions fare - well; I left my sweet
Jo - seph, though gone! The same hand that
D
whis - per I heard some - thing say, How
feel - ings, at rest is my soul, The
chil - dren (who for me do mourn) In
led me through scenes dark and drear Has
D Asus D
sweet - ly I sleep here a - lone!
tears are all wiped from my eyes.
far dis - tant re - gions to dwell.
kind - ly con - duc - ted me home.

Middlebury

In memory of Tim Rowe

Charles Wesley | Southern Harmony

G D
1. Come a - way to the skies. My be - lov - ed a -
2. Now with sing - ing and praise, let us spend all the
3. For the glo - ry we were first cre - a - ted to
4. We with thanks do ap - prove the de - sign of that
5. Hal - le - lu - jah we sing, to our Fa - ther and
G D
rise And re - joice in the day thou wast born;
days, by our hea - ven - ly Fa - ther be - stowed,
share, both the na - ture and king - dom di - vine!
love which hath joined us to Je - sus' Name;
King, and his rap - tu - rous prais - es, re - peat:
G C
On this fes - ti - val day, Come ex - ul - ting a -
while his grace we re - ceive from his boun - ty, and
Now cre - a - ted a - gain that our lives may re -
so u - ni - ted in heart, let us nev - er - more
to the Lamb that was slain, hal - le - lu - jah a -
G G C D G
way, And with sing - ing to Zi - on re - turn.
live to the ho - nor and glo - ry of God.
main, through - out time and e - ter - ni - ty Thine.
part, till we meet at the feast of the Lamb.
gain, sing, all hea - ven, and fall at his feet.

NATIVITY

IN HONOR OF PHIL SUMMERLIN

CHARLES WESLEY

THOMAS JARMAN

G C G D
1. GRACE. FOR A THOU - SAND TONGUES TO
2. HE BREAKS THE POW'R OF CAN - CELLED
3. MY GRA - CIOUS MAS - TER AND MY
4
G C D
SING MY GREAT RE - DEEM - ER'S PRAISE, MY
SIN, HE SETS THE PRIS - 'NER FREE; HE
GOD, AS - SIST ME TO PRO - CLAIM, AS -
7
G EMIN D A7 D
GREAT RE - DEEM - ER'S PRAISE,
SETS THE PRIS - 'NER FREE;
SIST ME TO PRO - CLAIM,
10
G C
THE GLO - RIES OF MY GOD AND
HIS BLOOD CAN MAKE THE FOUL - EST
TO SPREAD THRO' ALL THE EARTH A -
13
D G C
KING, THE TRI - UMPHS OF, THE TRI - UMPHS OF HIS
CLEAN, HIS BLOOD A - VAILED, HIS BLOOD A - VAILED FOR
BROAD THE HON - ORS OF, THE HON - ORS OF THY
16
G D BMIN
GRACE; THE TRI - UMPHS OF HIS GRACE, THE
ME; HIS BLOOD A - VAILED FOR ME, HIS
NAME; THE HON - ORS OF THY NAME, THE
19
C DSUS G
TRI - UMPHS OF HIS GRACE.
BLOOD A - VAILED FOR ME.
HON - NORS OF THY NAME.

New Britain

"Amazing Grace"

John Newton

Anonymous (Southern Harmony, 1835)

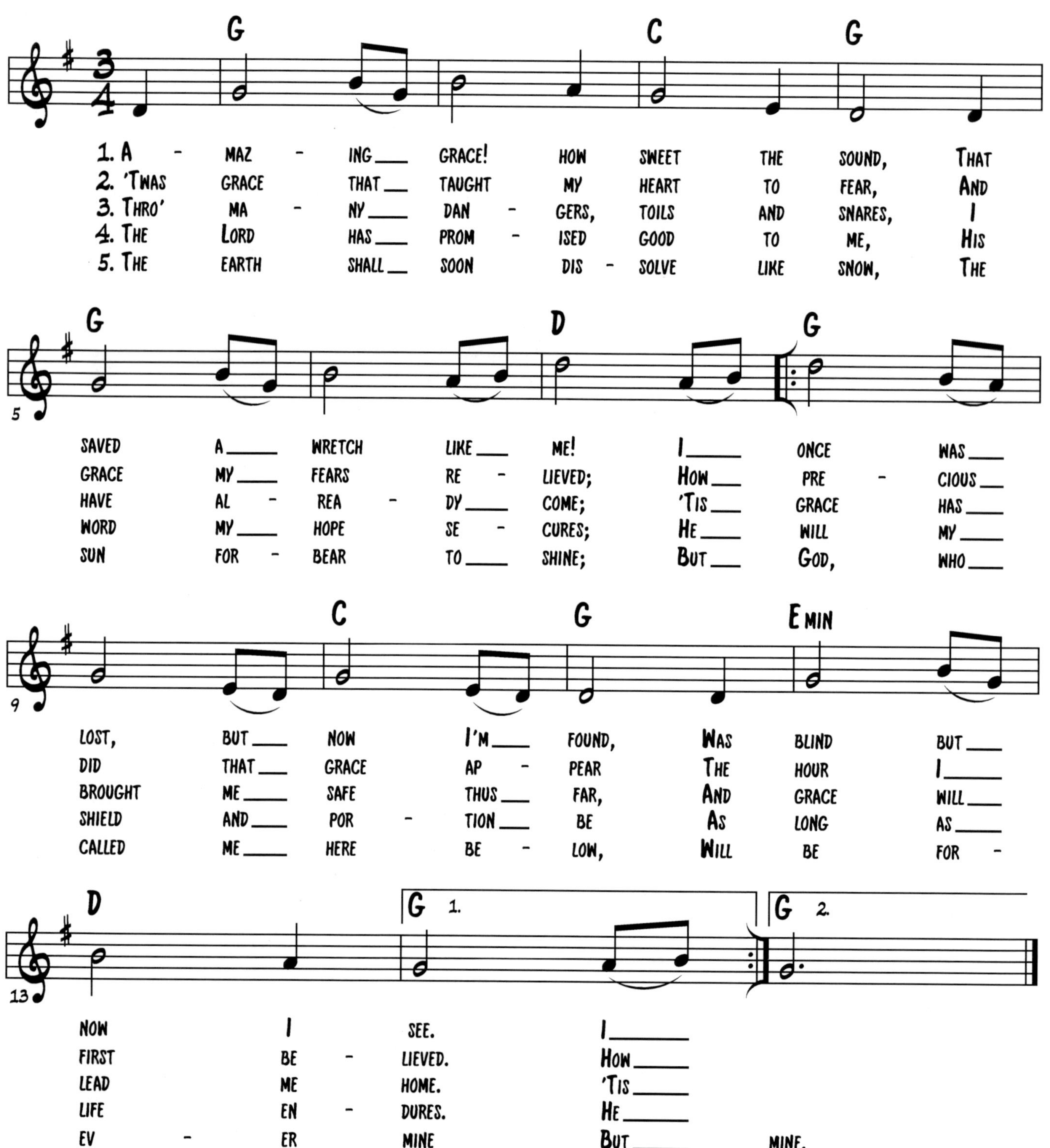

G C G
1. A - maz - ing grace! how sweet the sound, That
2. 'Twas grace that taught my heart to fear, And
3. Thro' ma - ny dan - gers, toils and snares, I
4. The Lord has prom - ised good to me, His
5. The earth shall soon dis - solve like snow, The
G D G
saved a wretch like me! I once was
grace my fears re - lieved; How pre - cious
have al - rea - dy come; 'Tis grace has
word my hope se - cures; He will my
sun for - bear to shine; But God, who
C G E min
lost, but now I'm found, Was blind but
did that grace ap - pear The hour I
brought me safe thus far, And grace will
shield and por - tion be As long as
called me here be - low, Will be for -
D G 1. G 2.
now I see. I
first be - lieved. How
lead me home. 'Tis
life en - dures. He
ev - er mine But mine.

O Come, Come Away

Southern Harmony

D G D
1. O come, come a - way! the Sab - bath morn is pass - ing; Let's
2. My com - rades in - vite to join their hap - py num - ber, And
3. While oth - ers may seek for vain and fool - ish plea - sures, The

G G A A
has - ten to the Sab - bath school; O come, come a - way! The
glad - ly will I meet them there; O come, come a - way! 'Tis
Sab - bath school shall be my choice; O come, come a - way! How

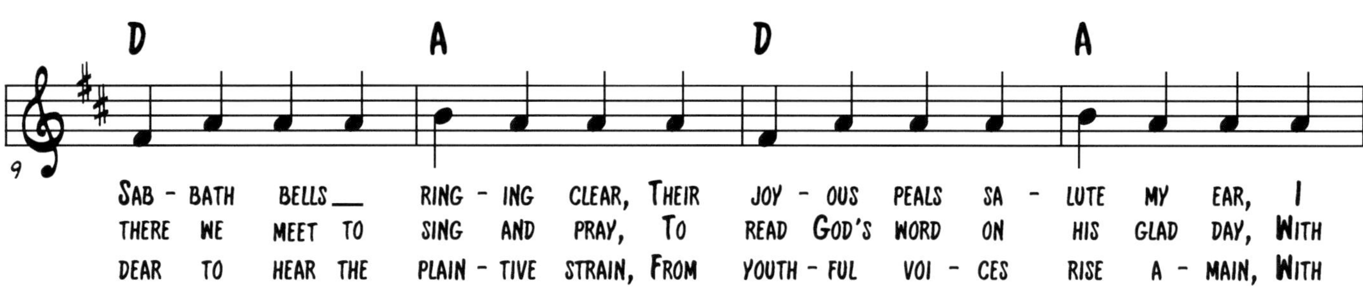
D A D A
Sab - bath bells ring - ing clear, Their joy - ous peals sa - lute my ear, I
there we meet to sing and pray, To read God's word on his glad day, With
dear to hear the plain - tive strain, From youth - ful voi - ces rise a - main, With

D A D A Asus D
love their voice to hear; O come, come a - way!
joy let's haste a - way, O come, come a - way!
sweet - est tones a - gain! O come, come a - way!

Promised Land

In memory of George E. Tutwiler

Lyrics: Peter B. Irvine

Miss Matilda T. Durham

E min
D
E min
B min
1. From here to hea - ven's well - built gates, all in a row they stand: they ___
2. Don't be im - pa - tient, so they say, though your pro - gress is slow. Just ___
3. For hea - ven's not a place to stay as in a clois - ter'd tow'r: It ___
4. So if you want to be with God as all of us ___ are now, just ___
E min
D
E min
are the ___ mar - tyrs and the saints, whose deeds o'er cent - 'ries span. They ___
take a ___ new step ev - 'ry day, and ___ pre - sent - ly you'll go to ___
is a ___ jour - ney and a way of ___ be - ing ___ here and now. We ___
fol - low ___ the same steps we trod when we the ___ Word did sow. Where ___
E min
D
E min
B min
lead the ___ way where we will stay when our life's work is done they ___
that coun - try ___ you long to see ___ where we make our ___ a - bode: to ___
find our ___ peace a - midst the strife of our life's ebb ___ and flow: We ___
e'er you ___ find God's will be done there's God's true self al - so Where ___
E min
D
E min
lead the ___ way where we will stay when ___ our life's work is done.
that coun - try you long to see where we make our a - bode.
find our ___ peace a - midst the strife of ___ our life's ebb and flow.
e'er you ___ find God's will be done there's God's true self al - so.

Quapaw

Charles Wesley

Thomas Commuck

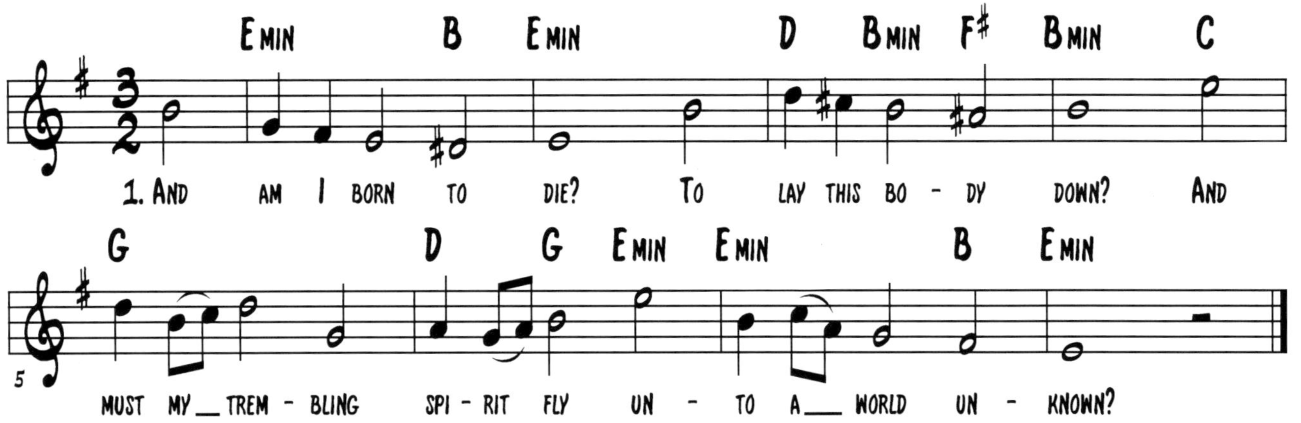

Emin B Emin D Bmin F# Bmin C
1. And am I born to die? To lay this bo - dy down? And
G D G Emin Emin B Emin
5
must my __ trem - bling spi - rit fly un - to a __ world un - known?

Restoration

In memory of Sue Blumer

Robert Robinson

William Walker, Compiler

Amin C G C G Amin
1. Come, thou font of ev - 'ry bless - ing Tune my heart to sing thy grace;
2. Teach me some mel - o - dious son - net, Sung by flam - ing tongues a - bove;
3. Oh to grace how great a debt - or, Dail - y I'm con - strained to be!
4. Prone to wan - der, Lord, I feel it; Prone to leave the God I love;

C G Amin G Amin
5
Streams of mer - cy, nev - er ceas - ing, Call for songs of loud - est praise.
Praise the mount, O fix me on it, Mount of God's un - chang - ing love.
Let thy good - ness like a fet - ter, Bind my wan - 'dring heart to thee.
Here's my heart, O take and seal it, Seal it for thy courts a - bove.

Amin C G C G Amin
9
I will rise and go to Je - sus, He'll em - brace me in his arms;
I will rise and go to Je - sus, He'll em - brace me in his arms;
I will rise and go to Je - sus, He'll em - brace me in his arms;
I will rise and go to Je - sus, He'll em - brace me in his arms;

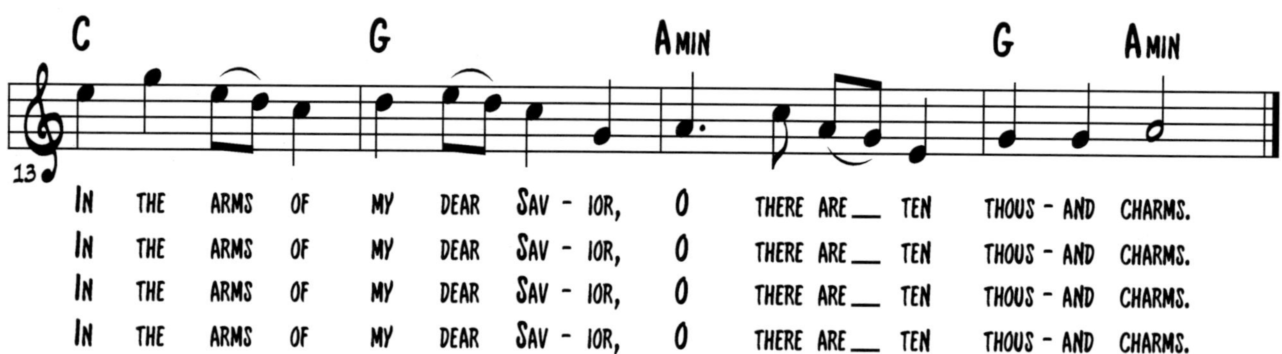
C G Amin G Amin
13
In the arms of my dear Sav - ior, O there are ten thous - and charms.
In the arms of my dear Sav - ior, O there are ten thous - and charms.
In the arms of my dear Sav - ior, O there are ten thous - and charms.
In the arms of my dear Sav - ior, O there are ten thous - and charms.

Star in the East

In memory of Phil A. Tabor

Reginald Heber

John B. Jackson

B min F♯min
1. Hail the blest morn, see the great Me - di - a - tor,
2. Cold on his cra - dle the dew - drops are shi - ning;
B min F♯min F♯min B min
Down from the re - gions of glo - ry des - cend!
Low lies his bed, with the beasts of the stall;
B min F♯min
Shep - herds, go wor - ship the babe in the man - ger,
An - gels a - dore him, in slum - bers re - clin - ing,
B min F♯min F♯min B min
Lo, for his guard the bright an - gels at - tend.
Wise men and shep - herds be - fore him do fall.
B min E min B min
Bright - est and best of the sons of the mor - ning!
Bright - est and best of the sons of the mor - ning!
B min E min F♯min
Dawn on our dark ness, and lend us thine aid;
Dawn on our dark - ness, and lend us thine aid;
B min F♯min
Star in the east, the ho - ri - zon a - dorn - ing,
Star in the east, the ho - ri - zon a - dorn - ing,
B min F♯min F♯min B min
Guide where our in - fant Re - dee - mer was laid.
Guide where our in - fant Re - dee - mer was laid.

Tender Thought

Thomas H. Kingo
Tr. Arthur J. Mason

A. Davisson, Kentucky Harmony

Emin D Emin A
1. O___ Je - sus, bless - ed Lord, to___ you My___
2. Break___ forth my soul, in joy and___ say: What___

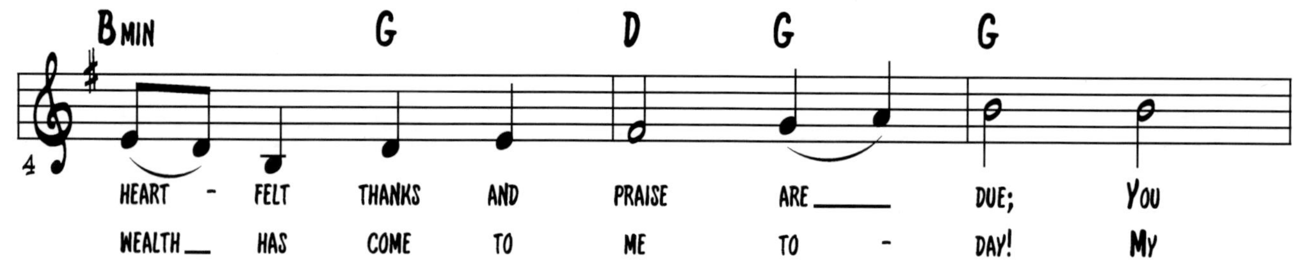

Bmin G D G G
4
heart - felt thanks and praise are___ due; You
wealth__ has come to me to - day! My

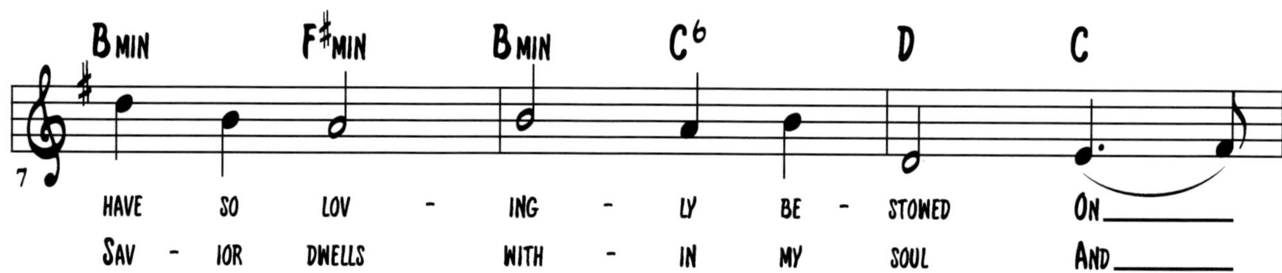

Bmin F♯min Bmin C6 D C
7
have so lov - ing - ly be - stowed On___
Sav - ior dwells with - in my soul And___

Bmin G F♯min D Emin
10
me___ your bod - y and your___ blood.
makes__ my wound - ed spi - rit___ whole!

Union

Thomas Baldwin

William Billings

Bmin F♯min
1. From whence does this un - ion a - rise, That
2. It can - not in E - den be found, Nor
3. My friends once so dear un - to me, Our
4. Sing Je - sus we e - ver shall reign, And
G F♯min Bmin D
4
ha - tred is con - quered by love? It fas - tens our
yet in par - a dise lost; It grows on Im -
souls so u - ni - ted in love: Where Je - sus is
all his bright glo - ry shall see, Sing - ing Hal - le -
A F♯min Bmin D
8
souls with such ties, That dis - tance and time can't re -
man - u - el's ground, And Je - sus' dear blood it did
gone we shall be In yon - der blest man - sions a -
lu jahs, A - men, A - men! e - ven so let it
Bmin D A F♯min
12
move. It fas - tens our souls with such ties, That
cost. It grows on Im - man - u - el's ground, And
bove. Where Je - sus is gone we shall be In
be! Sing - ing Hal - le - lu jahs, A - men, A -
Bmin D F♯min Bmin
16
dis - tance and time can't re - move.
Je - sus' dear blood it did cost.
yon - der blest man - sions a - Sing
men! E - ven so let it be.

Vernon

Charles Wesley

Azmi Chapin

Emin G Bmin
1. Come, O thou tra - ve - ler un -
2. I need not tell thee ___ who I ___
3. What though my shrink - ing ___ flesh com -
Emin D Emin
known, Whom still I hold, but can - not ___ see,
am; My ___ mi - se - ry and sin de - clare;
plain And ___ mur - mur to con - tend so ___ long,
Emin G Bmin
My com - pan - y be - fore is ___
Thy - self hast call'd me ___ by my ___
I rise su - pe - rior ___ to my ___
Emin D Emin
gone, And ___ I am left a - lone with ___ thee;
name, Look on thy hands and read it ___ there.
pain; When I am weak, then I am ___ strong?
G Emin Amin G
With thee all night I mean ___ to ___ stay, And
But who, I ask thee, who ___ art ___ thou? Tell
And when my all of strength ___ shall fail, I ___
Emin C D6 Emin Emin
wres - tle till the ___ break of day.
me thy name, and ___ tell me now.
shall with the God - man pre - vail.

Wayfaring Stranger

In honor of Deane Root

Adapt. Isaac Niswander

Arr. John M. Dye

1. I am a poor, way - fa - ring stran-ger, While jour-n'ying thru this world of woe, Yet, there's no
2. I know dark clouds will ga - ther o'er me, I know my way ___ is rough and steep; Yet beau - t'ous
3. I want to wear a crown of glo - ry, When I get home to that good land. I want to

sick - ness, toil nor dan-ger, In that bright land ___ to which I go. ___ I'm go-ing
fields ___ lie just be - fore me, Where God's re - deemed ___ their vi - gils keep. ___ I'm go-ing
shout ___ sal - va - tion's sto - ry, In Con - cert with ___ the blood-washed band. ___ I'm go-ing

there ___ to see my Fa - ther, I'm go - ing there ___ no more to roam; ___ I'm on - ly
there ___ to see my Mo - ther, She said she'd meet ___ me when I come; ___ I'm on - ly
there ___ to meet my Sav - ior, To sing his praise ___ for - e - ver more; ___ I'm on - ly

go - ing o - ver Jor - dan, I'm on - ly go - ing o - ver home. ___
go - ing o - ver Jor - dan, I'm on - ly go - ing o - ver home. ___
go - ing o - ver Jor - dan, I'm on - ly go - ing o - ver home. ___

Wondrous Love

In memory of Harry Lee Eskew

James Christopher

E min
E min
1. What won - drous love is this! oh, my soul! oh, my
2. When I was sink - ing down, sink - ing down, sink - ing
3. To God and to the Lamb, I will sing, I will
4. And when from death I'm free I'll sing on, I'll sing
B min
G
E min
D
E min
4
soul! What won - drous love is this! oh, my soul!
down, When I was sink - ing down, sink - ing down,
sing; To God and to the Lamb I will sing;
on, and when from death I'm free I'll sing on,
D
E min
G
8
What won - drous love is this That caused the Lord __ of
When I was sink - ing down Be - neath God's right - eous
To God and to the Lamb, Who is the great I
And when from death I'm free I'll sing and joy - ful
E min
E min
D
E min
12
bliss to bear the dread - ful curse for my soul, for my
frown Christ laid a - side His crown for my soul, for my
Am, While mil - lions join the theme, I will sing, I will
be, thro' - out e - ter - ni - ty I'll sing on, I'll sing
B min
G
E min
D
E min
16
soul, To bear the dread - ful curse for my soul.
soul, Christ laid a - side His crown for my soul.
sing, While mil - lions join the theme, I will sing.
on, thro' - out e - ter - ni - ty, I'll sing on.

About the Author

The Rev. Peter B. Irvine

Peter Irvine, AOJN is an Episcopal priest and musician, currently serving as Chaplain of the Association of Church Musicians (Madison Chapter AGO) in the Episcopal Diocese of Milwaukee. He has written many psalm paraphrases and original hymn texts, as well as hymn tunes. He attended Pittsburgh Theological Seminary for six years and completed a Master of Divinity from General Theological Seminary in 2002. He also earned a Bachelor of Arts and Doctor of Jurisprudence from the University of Tennessee, where he was born and lived until 1982. He plays piano, organ, harpsichord, guitar, mountain dulcimer and tin whistle, and especially enjoys music with a Celtic flavor. He worked with Harry Plantinga beginning in 1993 to create the online editions of Southern Harmony (a 19th century shape-note hymnal) and the 1916 Episcopal Hymnal on the Christian Classics Ethereal Library (CCEL), recording midi files for the more than 350 tunes in Southern Harmony. He also volunteers to enhance the hymnary.org database, with responsibility for hymnals of the Episcopal Church. He is an associate of the Order of Julian of Norwich (OJN), based in Antigo, Wisconsin, through which he met his wife Janet Marie Irvine, also an affiliate of OJN and a clinical psychologist.

Other Mel Bay Sacred Music Books